Contemporary Reflections

Contemporary Reflections

A COLLECTION OF VERSES THAT INSPIRE

Alka Vasudeva

PARTRIDGE

To order additional copies of this book, contact
Partridge India
000 800 10062 62
orders.india@partridgepublishing.com

www.partridgepublishing.com/india

Dedicated to

Omnipresent Omniscient Omnipotent
Lord Shiv incarnation Guruji

Foreword

Alka Vasudeva- A Birth Of Dawn.

In twentieth century the advent of English came with study of classical and modern literature and poetry of Dryden, Milton as classists and T. S Eliot, W B Yates etc as modern poets brought new concepts in Indian poetry. Though English poetry is not as prominent expressive form in India where Hindi classical and modern poetry of Vedas, Upanishads to our other regional Saints, Sufis poets and modern poets have their respectable place in hearts of Indian people but now globalization, our English poets has come forward to have their own impact in Indian society. In twentieth century science, social science and technology in modern fast changing society along with globalization has changed the mindset of society. Electronic media has also brought new changes and awareness about worldwide happenings. People are breaking chains of castes, creeds and old values to step in a diverse culture along with passion towards own healthy tradition.

In such scenario, the poetry of Alka Vasudeva, in Contemporary Reflections clearly shows impact of such changes. With her ardent desire, she advocates progressive and positive values in society and rejects old discarded values and thoughts which divided and are still dividing people. She is against discrimination and exploitation which is the cause of maladjustment, terrorism and wars on the Earth. She fearlessly analyzes and reflects what she feels from her heart about shortcomings of social system in our society. She is humanistic in thoughts and advocates human values, love and peace in her poetry tracing her thoughts though her subjective to objective approach.

As spurred by feelings and emotions while living in her socio-economic environment, she had divided her poetry in six different sections according content and matter diversification. In first section –Fun and Satire, her wit and satire make a reader smile when she talks of changing relations and new life style where from new born to mature people are run and fed by junk food instead of naturals and natural beauty is marred by artificial life style. Greed for luxurious life has brought mad run for attainments. Such way of materialistic life broke family system and individualism brought mutual relationship with duality or ivory shades of behavior in social and political life. This lead to anxiety, loneliness and uncertainty in life and she, in satirical way calls people as eco-warriors who came out from dark womb to darkness of their thoughts. She says that people are more anxious about phone changes thank keeping family intact calling it ;

> "We are eco warriors
> We believe in reuse"

Here comes the crisis of old v/s new generation contradiction added by crisis created by life styles by world trade and free marketing of newest gadgets .

In second section her romanticism sprouts our to give its fragrance in Rain and Love section where sensation of trickling rain creates love senses in flow of poetry and she beautifully illustrates;

> Earth feels pushes in its womb
> Rain baby is gaining growth
> Hopeful praying eyes
> Look towards heaven.

This brings in our mind prayers of people for rain in draught weather. While it brings love moments and sweet sensation of creativity in our mind, we are brought face to face of ruins of heavy rains and floods that bring misfortune ruins and rain becomes rain for eyes. Herein she puts live picture of children playing in rain and celebrates rain's rejuvenating effects. In this section while writing about changing relationship and fair weather friendships, she emphasizes that recklessness in relationship is treading under feet our long cherished spiritual and emotional entity. Still she is not devoid of serenity and sweetness of affections present in loving people when she celebrate moments of love with quotable lines ;

Love soothes
Through touch and smell of mother
Through bonds between siblings
Through service to humanity.
It mirrors in smiles
It beams in eyes
Love is pure pearl.

Then in third phase she writes about different relations of human being at different stages of life and outcome is odes to parenthood, marriage, brother sister, father, mother, doctors etc. Here she celebrates beauty and value of different relations.

In fourth section she offers cheers to soldiers who defend our land, patriots who suffer or suffered for freedom of our country. She celebrates free time but brings out wartime horror. Her salutation poems are to the soldiers and patriots who laid their lives to free and save out motherland. She observes that hate and discrimination lead to terrorism and wars and this takes lives of people of all ages.

In 5th section she writes about contradictions in life and compares their positive and negative roles as in day v/s night, love v/s hate, marriage v/s mirage etc and writes ode to Dhabas, on highways and allegorically concludes that when love is lost then comes the role of divinity and morality;

Lust is selfish
Love is selfless
Lust chases
Love rests
Lust leads to obsession
Love leads to salvation
Lust leads to sulking
Love leads to caring.

In this part using analogy in her poetics, she asks readers to stick to selfless love and service to lead a life of real bonds of passion and enjoy beauty in diversity of cultures and advocates role of gyms, library, e-books, CDs etc to inculcate multi Cultural values.

In concluding section being a true Indian culture model, her mystic and metaphysical belief writes about spiritual and divine values which are basis of Indian culture. Having faith in spirituality and divinity and as a true devote of Shiva and The Buddha, she writes devotional poetry. Here she also wants to inculcate in readers that success too is time bound as colors of a rainbow. She takes nature and its beauty as source of joy and pleasure as she happily behold beauty and grace in trees, flowers, moon and stars, sun,sea, rivers like the Ganga, In this part of her book, soft corner of the woman in her is exhibited . She writes poetry with feelings and emotions which only a woman can scribble beautifully and she has done it motherly, with naturalistic and impressionistic way and she is true picture of Indian Culture. Only she can say that a little gesture is big relief, a smile and soft touch can cause wonders, solace and healing. In her allegorical poetry as in War Against Cancer, her concern about suffering humanity and its causes shakes our minds to rise against such evils. Her poetry brings out her caring and humanistic attitude which is the need of the time. Her optimism sprouts out flowers of different colors and scents in dessert of pessimism.

Giving analytical analysis of her poetry and poetic diction, I appreciate techniques which she used to beautify her poetry. She used appropriate metaphors, illustrations, connotations, alliterations, personifications, visionary and picturesque effects along with historical and mythological references, rhythmic flow and rain like showers of didactic insertions. She also used dialogic and analogical style in her poetry to exhibit dramatic impact. Her poetry is capable of creating sensations and vibrant emotional vibes by her informal and conveying way of expression. I am sure her poetry will inculcate her optimistic attitude and philosophy as well as inherited and acquired heritage of Indian culture. Welcoming her dawning advent, I wish her success and I am sure readers will relish her poetry.

It. Amen!

California, U S A
6th Feb.2017

Mohinderdeep Grewal

Chairperson World Association of English Poetry,
Ex Gen Secretary Kendri Punjabi Lekhak Sabha (Reg.)

Expression of Gratitude

To my revered Guru Ji I owe a lot.

Without His blessings life is rudderless.

I could have not even thought of getting this collection of poems published.

Secondly I am indebted to my reader friends on the social media site Face book as they were the ones to encourage as well as suggest getting the poems composed impromptu to be given a book form. The words of appreciation by renowned poet Monhinderdeep Grewal, Colonel Amardeep Singh, Ex. Wing Commander Ved Prakash Sachar and Session judge Mrs. Reema Malhotra Sachdeva boosted my creativity a lot.

I am indebted to my family and friends who made me realize the fact that my words inspired positivity in those who read. Special thanks Mr. Mahesh Kaul from Jammu, who took the time out to read and suggest edits in this compilation. There are many more whom I owe my gratitude for being the silent supporters. Last but not the least I do thank the team under Mr. Pohar Baruah to skillfully present my verses in the book form.

Dear Readers

Poetry for me has always been the art of using diction in a style that ignites the minds and soothes the souls. It has been a medium to paint through words. Words have always been springing spontaneously sensing the inward as well as outwardly catalysts.

"Contemporary Reflections" is not an academic volume but the compilation of my sensitivities that pulsated in my consciousness as a human being in different roles during my life time. Be it a teacher or mother, family holder or a responsible Indian citizen.

This compilation of poems written over a period of time is like a wave that has crests and troughs as life is not a static phenomenon however an ever dynamic process has its own momentum. Aesthetics of life; both animate and inanimate have been integral to my expressions.

I have tried to segment each aspect of life that had an effect on me and thus presented my collection of poems in such a way. I have a firm faith that my readers will relate to my experiences as their own. After all human life is same though locale and conditions may vary.

The various sections of my collection titled 'Contemporary reflections are as follows:

- ➢ **Fun and Satire**
- ➢ **Rain and Love**
- ➢ **Relationships and Psyche**
- ➢ **Patriotism and Valor**
- ➢ **Comparison and Description**
- ➢ **Faith, Philosophy and Contemporary**

I hope "Contemporary Reflections" having myriad issues in its content will make readers identify themselves with the events and episodes. And you ponder how Divine and Cosmic this life is.

Wish you a happy reading!

Alka Vasudeva

Fun & Satire

Unusual Guest!

Just yesterday in hot June afternoon
Entered in Vikas Chopra's chamber a rat couple for honeymoon
He was reading an important mail on his PC
They were roaming in his vicinity like enjoying at Washington DC

When he placed his foot down from the footrest
The experience for him was the craziest
Toast of their married life rat couple had celebrated
His Woodland shoes were now much more ventilated

He summoned his staff for an urgent meeting
To treat the couple in the manner befitting
Problem was discussed at length
It was decided to install supersonic wavelength

Immediately net was explored
All tactics to tackle their menace implored
Vikas announced a decision very bold
"Killer of them will get a gram of gold", in the meeting he told.

The rat couple enjoyed all uproar
They then went from their honeymoon destination through restroom floor
They were the most unusual guest
They are known to be cutest pest

Stress had an impact but their love was intact.

The clock struck six
Both of them felt themselves in a fix.
"O my God
Again no time!
Be fast." he spoke aloud as he could.
He started brushing his teeth as fast as he could.
Toothpaste tasted to his tongue different
He instantaneously spat the foam non repentant
He rinsed his mouth hurriedly sensing tight time.
Haste makes waste.
He learnt post putting shaving cream in place of tooth paste!

Witnessing from kitchen was his wife.
She was in bout of laughter in his time of strife.
"Men are men, they won't use sense", mockingly said his wife.

"Get ready soon
O madam come out fast from your beauty salon!"
Irritated husband spoke then.
Wife smiled with confidence.
She gulped breakfast, took her handbag.
The last touch was left.
In dim light
She took the deodorant canister
Sprayed on herself the madam home minister
Fuming with anger
Hubby waiting outside in their car
Started laughing loud

Madam well dressed
In time stress
Had actually sprayed
On herself
In place of sweet sensuous deodorant
She sprayed strong smelling pain relief
So urban fast paced life
Stress had an impact
But sense of humor
Kept their love intact

April 03 2012, 3 pm

The tussle of a different kind!

It started with a beautiful color combination
Amid initial discussion
Number One decided to bake the cake.
Number Nine got thrilled with piping design
Both got ready with their tools
The aroma of the sponge made many in neighborhood salivate
The creamy colors caught concentration
Now started the tussle of a different kind
Baker ruled by number one
Always finds ways to outshine
Crazy artist ruled by number nine
Tries to surpass with artfully done creamy piping
The tussle delivered many delicious cakes
And will keep doing so in future too
Till the ultimate winner is declared
Number one carries the creative trait
Tries different recipes and mixes unique tastes
Number Nine pitches perfection in each creation
Designing becomes happy celebration
Those who savior their yummy dishes
Applaud the efforts but
Hardly know the ongoing tussle of different kind.
Interestingly both the numbers make people crazy
With One the counting starts and
With nine when one blends
Then another series starts
In between them
From two to eight
All numbers for their say have to wait

‖ *Hats off to Double Standards in India!*

From crimson shaded Sunrise
to silvery soothing shine of Moonrise
In the lanes and by lanes
across the states
Eyes catch the glimpses many!!
With break of dawn
Men, Women, Children
can be seen
sitting and shitting.
Be it a State or National highway.
It makes no difference.
There must be a veil /burqa indeed
Cover the face
Does it matter then who sees your ass?
Leave the talk of shit aside.
Few of cops without helmet do ride!
Does it matter for a beaconed vehicle if the road is narrow or wide!
A little space...a bike can skid zig zag even on the wrong side!!
Right under the sign of No smoking
Bollywood poster glamorizes smoking like act divine!!
Across all parties and religions
Moral brigade is always ready
for full ho hulla!!
All morality doses poured on girl child!
There is larger than life gender divide!!
Girls' dress and dressing sense attracts attention and moral brigade's fine!!
And in all metro markets female lingerie is sold by male seller is
absolutely morally fine!!!
We respect the females it is our cultural entity.
Using female anatomy to abuse is Masculine identity!!!
Female is worshipped as Deity
but in real life she is supposed to be fully domestic!!
Girl is groomed as family pride.

Instead of giving an equal share
she is paid Dowry as Bribe!!
In a land where resources are less and population more
Dowries are used as tool to settle score!!
Karma theory is followed less and discussed more!!
Karma called the action is labeled Right or Wrong!
But Honor hardly debited or credited in the Karmic account!!
If teased or molested
all good Karma and integrity for the victim diminishes!
The acquittals show how the culprits easily exit from the clutches!
Fish in aquarium taken good care,
Fish in rivers not allowed living free.
Double standards are visible everywhere
Latest attitude is "Who cares."

What an Irony!

We grew there from single cell to full grown baby.
We all swam happily in fluid filled dark dungeon.
We ate through her.
We saw through her.
We breathed through her.
We felt the world through her.
Now
To live we want spacious Villa in Washington DC.
To breathe we need a window or split AC.
To connect with world we need Apple I-phone or a Windows 7 PC.
To feel safe we need services of an ADC.
To understand the world around we learn ABC.
To feed bellies we need Pasta, Sushi, Manchurian,
Oriental, Chinese, Mughlai, Thai, and Indian filling to CC (cold coffee).
For months we grew in fluid filled dark womb.
But now facing dark makes many dumb.
Darkness infused light of life.
Darkness taught us to swim smooth in strife.
We dread it now the most.
We try to figure in it a nonexistent Ghost.
We forget to cheer in its name a toast ¡¡¡

May 17, 2012

Love letters are customized!

When Eve ate forbidden apple
she left her Adam
Draping on her the maple leaves
Adam realized his pain.
The warmth of his heart,
The message of his love,
he did send through exhaling in Air.
When the wind touched his Eve
It conveyed the Adam's love notes indeed.
Cycle of time moved fast
Now civilest Ape
Knew how to drape and how to scribble
His courier of love
Became that white dove
Faithfully the bird
Kept on doing his duty
For centuries
To unite the separated lovers
Sincerely delivering letters to beauty.
With dawn of Postal service
Boys started sending the scented floral printed page
they took days to sigh
their calligraphies scripted soulful emotions.
The postman could from miles estimate the lovers' warmth.
The letter box was opened hundred times a day.
Wheel of time wheeled new dimension
Now the lovers were calling each other sitting far in their mansion.
O! Nears and dears could hear
When they talked in whispers

Mobile phones out from the packed box
Snatched privileged position of the postbox
Love birds shifted to inbox.
Smiles added on their faces
many messages per hour were in the traces
Adam just sent warmth
Eve felt the emotion
Now Adam can woo many Eves using forwarded texts
Kisses are attached like accessories
Eves are equally happy
Charging their phone bills
By new boy friend
Love letters are customized
21 century lovers are very wise.

24 June 2012-

What a Crisis!

When the attention of the media is on act of ISIS
Metropolitan young is writing another thesis!
In the age of smart phones
which should be the ring and caller tune?
Choosing a meal is still easy
but boggles mind to choose a phone that is a class!
Samsung S5 or NOTE2 or Micromax Canvas!
HTC or LG or Sony Xperia
Which one is cool!
The computer expert is called and consulted.
RAM
PROCESSER
FEATURES are discussed.
Is this phone worth for taking a Selfie?
Tons of messages with friends exchanged.
Millions of websites on Google explored.
The efforts make the elders think
Is it a search for a gadget or some treasure?
The peer pressure is paramount!
Mobile phone is not a mere gadget.
Among peers it's your Status count!
A meeting in person to cousins and friends can be ditched
but for comments a selfie with even a statue at a Mall is clicked!
A small sleek Mobile catches more attention.
Wow! What brand! What Price!
All in the group discuss Clock and Anti clockwise.
"Is your one water and dust resistant?
"Share with me the picture quality".
"Download games the open Play store."

"What's your BBM pin?"
"Add me on what's app."
The crisis does not end here.
Now the hunt starts for accessories.
It makes us wonder how without thunder
Mobile phone has invaded in lives and space!

22 June 2014-

We are Eco Warriors!

We are Eco warriors.
We believe in Reuse.
Amrita Singh divorced her hubby and career.
By Karenna Saif is happy to be for Reused.

We are Eco warriors.
We believe in Recycle.
In an apartment in Guru Gram
A couple earning gold in milligrams
They left their son in care of a maid
They watched her moves on CCTV footage.
The maid was left under the supervision of terrier.
But one day she used her urine surely as water **recycled.**

We are Eco warriors.
We believe in Reduce.
Whether it is the summer of Rajasthan
Or it is the snow clad Himalayan range
Bollywood divas wear minimum on when on shooting stage.
They spread awareness on expenses on wardrobe to be **reduced.**
We are Eco warriors.
We believe in Refuse.
In doing so our leaders feel superior
during summer's public may sweat a lot but continuous electricity supply
is **refused.**
We are Eco warriors.
We do not believe in Wastage.
We follow the motto
Reuse Recycle Reduce Refuse.

3 July 2012

Don't you know it is in fashion?

The sweet sixteen was their age.
With their attire they tried to burn the carriage.
They were for sure from affluent background.
They wore branded footwear,
This did not screech or sound when they stepped in or stride around.
An elderly lady just could not be resolute
Asked the young guys why denims were torn above their feet?
Her sympathy to them turned out to be a taunt
It was the fashion brand denim they were trying to flaunt.
Controlling agony they in reply asked this question
"Don't you know it is in fashion?"
Now it was the lady's turn to feel awkward
Educated but still was she in her fashion sense backward?
The world of celluloid flashed fast in her memory
She recalled how cinema has been promoting fashion accessories.
The tie, the bow, the belts, the shoe,
The handbags and hair bands keep changing trend.
Fashion magazines do sell like hot cakes on the stands.
Fashion has now reached an all time soaring.
Fad is now in tattoo and body piercing.
Hairs too are not spared.
Either they are bonded or colored.
For nails the art specialists exist.
Tempting designs and colors no one can resist.
Mother's Care has entered as craze.
For infants they carry beautiful range.
Their dresses, bibs, socks too rock.
With all this awakening she was in shock.
The carriage halted with smooth jerk
She did exit with words echoing in her mind
This sentence seemed be on auto rewind
"Don't you know it is in fashion?"

Our Ivory Shades

Elephant thou art not alone
To have duality in use of teeth
In our conduct we Indians do duality hone
We hide our true colors beneath shining sheath

Our Gods are very strange
From Matsaya avatar to Stove devta is the range
Their deformities are a blessing divine
A child born with such deformity is on the parents and society a divine fine!!!!

Full of luxury and entertainment is Heaven
Lords enjoying dancing damsels sipping golden goblets of Somras
Numerous God men also enjoy luxuries lives worth star seven
A woman for survival when a dance in a bar is treated like carcass!!!!

In the Land of Spirituality we preach for others life of Austerity
Gripping too firmly the Superstitions
Filling the coffers of God and hundreds of God men in the name of Charity
Numerous are compelled to sleep hungry shelter less without human
considerations!!!!

We believe two philosophies of ADVAIT and DVAIT
Advaits say God and its creation are no different but both are one
Dvaits say Creator and creations are not one
Followers play opportunist, philosophies are twisted and in practice we
deviate!!!!

Just like thou O Elephant!
We do not show our real teeth
Outwardly we blow different Trumpet
We hide our true colors beneath shining sheath.

What would PEOPLE say?

A few seconds back
on the timeline of my Face book friend.
This phrase got posted in colloquial, "Log kya kahenge?"
Translation tool converts the phrase, **"What would People say?"**
In an instant
This makes happiness flee from our lives away.
People tend to live in unidentified fear.
They think a lot before they wink their eyes.
All thanks to this notorious phrase, **"What would People say?"**
Pleasure is in buying a movie ticket
Happiness is in sitting cross legged on cinema hall seat!
But it gets ruined courtesy **"What would People say?**
He/ She forget for movie tickets he/she paid and not the **PEOPLE.**
Pleasure is enjoying the walk in rain.
Happiness lies in jumping on every poodle while rain walking on the way.
"What would People say?" blocks the happiness anyway.
Pleasure is enjoying the company of friends.
Happiness lies in loud laughter and free gesture in between friendly talks.
But here too **"What would People say?"** stalks happiness on the way.
Pleasure is buying an ice-cream on hot summer noon
Happiness is licking the ice-cream with big tongue coming out
"What would People say?" keeps tongue in and Happiness kicked out.
Pleasure and Happiness remain together only
when I write willfully accepting views
as it becomes a tool
to know
"What would People say?"

March 13, 2014, 11:54 pm

Rain & Love

Pitter patter! Pitter patter!

The date is 29 November again.
The clouds seem busy with in bargain!
Pitter patter! Pitter patter!
This is the rain soon be served as winter's chilled starter!
So beautiful are going to be foggy mornings!!!
Flyover would become the runway.
Our cars the air car!
Bright colors pep up with smoky breath!!!
Season to sip soups and gorge sizzlers!!!!
Hot babes heating the hot coffee!!!
Around bone fire night watchmen chewing tobacco toffee!!
Some get their nose stuffy!!
Moms make kids wear woolens fluffy!!!
Pitter patter pitter patter
this is the rain soon be served in winter's chilled starter!!!
Soft mink blankets or
Cotton quilts beat Lux cozy
Snuggling in softness.
Heavenly becomes the soft burrow!!
Warmth of affection adds to it.
Pitter patter pitter patter
this is the rain soon be served in as winter's chilled starter!!

November 29, 2015

Lovers: the Earth and Sky

She takes those deep sighs.
He showers the kisses.
Her agony raises the heat.
He in passion uproots the trees.
Their love to our eyes is a blissful treat.
Afterwards Sky adds Rainbow to glorify her beauty.
Their long distance relationship,
they are truly honestly maintaining
Across the Globe their love is worshipped!!!
Man can reach Moon.
He can spend millions on Honeymoon.
Still he can never match and catch the zenith of the Sky's love.
She too can never match and catch the zenith of the Earth's patience!!!
Our eyes keep waiting to see them mating!

ℛain ℛrofile

Ugly Sun ogles
somewhere deep under the Mediterranean
Earth feels the pushes
in its womb
Rain baby is gaining growth.
Hopeful praying eyes
Look towards heaven.
Prayers answered.
Thirsty souls welcome.
The touch is magical.
The First raindrops touch.
Pleasant like that of a New Born baby!
Everyone wants to get a hug and it enchants all!
Rain infancy passes soon.
In Childhood, it plays truant.
It is in playful mood of hide and seeks.
It rains in Southern part
Western remains dry.
Teasing clouds appear and move without shower.
With lightening thunder, it announces its Young blood
loud noisy noticeable downpour almost everywhere.
As Youth turns violent
so does the Rain.
In cities on roads, it creates chaos and watery potholes.
Aggression of Rain goes high
it ravages with flood.
The seasonal and perennial rivers swell.
On Earth Rain creates hell.
The Uncontrollable
Then cools down.
It pours still but less vigor.
Perfectly matches the Middle age.
Rain is consistent without rage.

Now its presence a charm does not trigger.
Colder winds start blowing.
Dryness on the skin increases.
Rain has entered the unwanted Old Age!
People, who had prayed for its birth in the month of May,
Now pray again in October for its end anyway.
They get ready to bid it the farewell.
With one or two falls here and there,
it finally goes to Rest in Peace.
It waits to Reborn.

Rainy flavors of life

With arms wide open
Running across the road like a butterfly
Road beneath got gradually polka dotted
Lane was filled with carefree giggling gang of butterflies
All felt powerful at not getting wet
Its sweetest flavor Strawberry passed
With childhood
Clouds gathered again
Dark black
Wind brought the urge to meet someone special
Suddenly both remembered
That was the best time
To go to get that wind chime urgently repaired
Clothes got wet
But they enjoyed they met
Umbrella one
But they were two
How long it kept raining
They had no clue
It was the Cherry Chocolate flavor
That with adolescence got over
The wheel of time moved
the two of them
got married
now rain
Poured again
the air aroused them
in that thunderous lightening
Heavy downpour
just like the tendril and tree
they mingled free
Inseparable they were
like raisins from Rum and Raisins flavor

Rained it then
Rains it now
It enchanted then
It depresses now
The dark clouds
Freshens the memory of that shroud
Cruel destiny snatches
One of the love birds die
Rain is the flood from eyes
Its named Lemon and Lime flavor
Rain that dampened the loner
Nurtures the ground
New generation grows giggling
Grand parent bonding with grand children
Souls immerse in joy
Watching
Part of own body and souls
Chasing the polka dotted roads
Reliving through them that butterfly pride
Sense of sight hearing and smell gone weak
Wrinkled smiles fondly watch drizzle
Sharing stories stroking affectionately grandchildren
This is the fragrant French Vanilla
Leaving in air essence forever

July 16, 2012

Karma Preacher Rain

Birds and Beasts
Trees and Toddlers
All enjoy the drops of mercy
It is the Karma Preacher Rain indeed.

Trees offering shade and fruit
Trees standing tall and straight
Not all of them get watered by man indeed
They stand in the scorching Sunlight
Provide relief to those nestling in their branches
Provide flowers and fruits to all without any grouse.
When the leaves turn golden and whither
The God up in heavens then downpours with mercy!

Those who study the plant life they say
In thanks giving to God the trees in rain sway.
They keep whole life sucking water from under the ground
They keep exhaling oxygen for all to inhale.
They have no claim on the fruits of their Karma.
They have to bear the pain when woodpecker hits on the stem.
They have to bear the load of children enjoying swings hung with rope on the branches.
For decades and centuries these big trunk trees
Pay penance for the Bad Karmic account perhaps.
They wait and wait for ultimate salvation.
With mercy of Divine in each thunder storm few get liberated when uprooted!

Rain brings smile on the face of Humanity.
Rain allows the flowers to bloom.
Rain rejuvenates the field for farmers around the globe.
Rain is awaited to reward the sweat shed by the farmers.
Rain is worshipped to carry her blessings brimming through the rivers.
Rain shower on the Water Day
Confirms the existence of Hope and Humanity

When it rains in school

Seasonal breaks are a trend across globe
Post the vacations children buy new school wardrobe
Be the students going to school in India
Or somewhere as far as in Indonesia
How much they love rain is not the matter of discussion
Drenching in the divine shower is always in fashion
Parents escort lovingly holding umbrellas in one hand
Keeping the hold on the lovely blood of their own with other hand
Some escort till the bus stand
Others make to drive and drop till the school bend
Bubbling Chirping Shining Smiling faces
Some stopping at stairs to tie their shoe laces
Looking up above in the sky
They wave to say hello to friends flying by
Some wearing neatly ironed school dress
With their smile teachers they impress
Spending summer vacations enjoying great chill
Getting graded Holidays Homework is task uphill
They look for an excuse
Their water filled flying friends darken classes to their rescue
"Its dark now.
O Teacher! We can see the board how?"
Suddenly some seek for washroom permission
Getting wet in downpour is their mission
With their drenched dresses
They excite others to ask for outdoor passes
In some rooms rain feels noisy
While in some overall look is messy
Chhapak chhapak chhapak
Its the sound that stalk
Teachers balance books, looks and umbrella to walk
Chhapak chhapak chhapak
Nursery kids are shown rain

Senior ones mug up with studies plain
Canteen contractor does not let go rain in vain
Sensing the impact
He fills saliva drooling in air in fact
Of hot Samosas Bread Pakoras Coffee and Masala tea again and again
Most enjoyable in the school
Its Rain!Rain!Rain!

Friends of Different Hues

Circumstances play prism to bring out friendship hues
Those who grew up together
They not necessarily are birds of the same feather
One may be energetic extrovert
Other may be totally opposite cool introvert
Their bond is like blending red with blue.
Circumstances play prism to bring out friendship hues
Friends who played in school studying together.
They could be living away in different set ups altogether.
One might have enjoyed schooling as a smooth ride.
The other might have carried school bag with slowly stride.
One might have never been writing assignments.
The other might have found in notebooks writing merriment.
Their bond is like blending pink with blue.
Circumstances play prism to bring out friendship hues
Friends who played pranks in college on others.
They could possibly join same job together.
One could be picked up on merit through campus selection.
The other could get a chance on friend's recommendation.
Their bond is like adding silver with blue.
Circumstances play prism to bring out friendship hues
Those who are added in life through others
They may continue to be sailing mutely together
One may be a sort of leader
Other could be the ardent admirer
Their bond is like adding dew drop on blue.
Circumstances play prism to bring out friendship hues
Those who are chosen by family or matrimony broker
They could keep sailing in hope to change each other
One may be dominant
Other may be dormant
Their bond is like adding water drops to blue.

August 6, 2016, 12:24 p.m.

All weather friends.

In their diaper days,
whenever one cried,
the other cried louder.
Tossing turning in their cradles,
They looked at each other eye to eye.
Smile to smile they exchanged.

From cradle to the day they could crawl
Their bond of friendship also got strength small.

"Please send my friend to the play ground."
Both used the same plea and sentence.
Their moms as expected responded, "School assignment still not fully
done...you can go alone to ground."
With head drooping downward
The friend would walk two paces forward.
With faster speed he turns around.
He pounces on the friend like grey hound.
After initial exchange of kicks and blows,
He joins hands to decrease his assignment work load.

These friends entered in troublesome teens together.
Both of them always fought a lot.
They argued and giggled together.
They became friends for all weather.
They hated each other's personality trait.
They attacked each other's critic like krait.
But still they were the best playmates.
Any idea that would strike in one's mind
The other buddy would execute without mind.
Mom, Dad, Neighbors, Bro and Sis
On their strong bond, all of them got pissed

Distances, Responsibilities, Family and Job liabilities
Never mattered and marred for each other their availability.

Mystical it is to understand their bond.
They do not get time to meet.
Daily within their hearts best wishes they always greet.

From diaper days through troubling teens,
From school day life to earning hand,
From bachelorhood to marriage band,
Life takes them together touch the old age.
Now even their love has craze.
Whenever together they sit and smile,
their gossips go as long as river Nile.
Their tales of being each other's strength
Their tales of firm faith on each other,
The anecdotes of their life,
Inspire their children and grandchildren.

Romance is a sweet dessert in life.

Bollywood or Hollywood
Or it can be any cinema wood.
Romance is portrayed and sold.
On screen
A hero and a heroine
Start getting enchanted towards each other.
They do have deep sighs.
They are a cajoling pair.
They have twinkling prying eyes.
They always part bodily.
Their souls remain bonded.
In movies
ice cream vender has always full stock
but they share for sharing is caring!!!
Love birds tweet.
Heroine is always sweet
Hero is always hard nut outside.
Initially they both are ready to fight.
Then affection bites them mid fight.
Romance in life is bit different.
Eye to eye lovers say a lot.
Ages pass without an open talk.
Parents, peers put pressure
no outsider can their love measure.
Romance is more in
playing hide and seeks of emotions.
Some enjoy public affection
others are happy in getting silent acceptance.
Romance was,
Romance is and
Romance will be a sweet dessert in life.

Beauty of Bond

Just last night
some words by someone
triggered a thought.
What is so special in the bond
that is marital?
Is it the passion session
that carries them to unison?
Is it the kids that bond them together?
Is it the trust that grows each day?
Is it all sweet or the spices exists too?
The smiles
the caresses
the cuddles
are all the sugar content.
But they come after gulping
the chilly taunts
the heated discussions
the long absence
Thus underlies in the routine silly fights
the fathom deep hold of the sweetness
Man and Woman
enjoy till eternity the physical, emotional and spiritual connection
which is full on spices and sweetness of affection.
They gradually become each other's need
they gradually add to each other's boredom.
They gradually accept each other's freedom.
Man and Woman
enjoy till eternity the physical, emotional and spiritual connection.

October 18, 2015, 4:04 pm

Love lies in the eyes of beholder.

Daily we may not meet
Daily we may not greet
We may live miles away
We may not recall each day
But when their comes a tempest
We are there to do for each other the best
This bond of love and trust
Proves emotions do not rust
True bonds survive
Beyond the barriers of border
Resist together the tempest just like big boulder
Shakespeare said beauty lies in the eyes of the beholder
I say love lies in the soul of the beholder

Love is Pure Pearl

Sitting by the side of window
Eyes captured
All in the range
Across the road focused
On the lush green park in front
Trees swaying shinning crown
A man walking like a clown
Oldies sitting in one corner
Children rubbing jostling
Chasing giggling
Flowers and dresses splashing color
Vibrancy in air
Under the shade
A couple unmindful
Of the world around in the ground
Held each other passionately
Oldies passing at them stares
Children were unaware
Just then
Thought struck
Is it love or lust?
Love is pearl
Hidden deep inside
Away from the selfish world
Sunrays reach but not the heat
Oyster protects it in shell

Love soothes
- through the touch and smell of mother
- as bond between siblings
-as trust between friends
- through service to humanity.
It mirrors in smile.
It beams in eyes.
Love is pure pearl.

May 05, 2012

Will I Be Ever Loved???

Loyalty
Obviously
Vociferates
Emotions
This LOVE exists in abundance
Parents and Pets shower unconditional.
Friends and Siblings believe in reciprocation.
Enemies believe in provocation.
Those who snatch it are Attention Seekers
still many complain
WILL I BE EVER LOVED????

Man and Woman Can Be Well Wishers

Man and Woman can be well wishers
Man loves to play big brother
Even if younger
Woman loves to take care
Even if she is in cradle chair
Both love being together
Both think poles apart
They stand for each other
As father or father figure
As mother or mother figure
As doting brother or sister
As husband wife they face each strife
In offices can be good colleagues
But unfortunately
The pious relation of FRIEND
Is not accepted in between
Is it Society?
Or
is it gene of Romancing?
Friend gets classified as Boy Friend or Girl friend
why is this trend?
Why can't a Friend be just Friend?
Why add Gender identity as toxicant the Divine bond called Friend?

22 January 2015, 7:16 pm

Relationship & Psyche

Marriage: Mission to Change.

With the birth starts the wait
an innocent infant listens in cradle
Lullaby filled with
Dream of marrying dream boy or dream girl!!!
Nursery admissions a challenge
Not for being literate but
"Learned and well settled can get the best groom or bride"
Adolescence puts family in oblivion
Infatuation reaffirms the chase for dream partner
Youth is fortified and targeted
Parents Peers
All near and dears
Wire web of dream life ahead
Without life partner
Its shown a road dead end!!!
Spell bound the young hearts
Romeo Juliet
Start searching each other
in new century in a new way
Now on Face book and Twitter
the love interest kindles as sweeter!!!!
The hunt closes when
Parents choice or
Self choice
binds together girls and boys
Marriage then becomes
Mission to change.

Ode to Parenthood

Though we Hindus are teased world over
For dedicating each of 365 days to celebration
Still I found United Nations adopting our concept to fulfill some missions
First June is dedicated as Global Parents Day!

At first I thought it as market driven celebration
As at Archie's stores we can see
Cards and many more gift items for so many occasions and days
Mother's Day
Father's Day
Sister's Day
Brother's Day
Friendship Day
The list is so big in a way.

Since 2012 the day saw the light of jubilation
In rapidly developing nations surely raised the need to honor Parenting.
When toddlers are left in the care of baby sitters
When mother and father connect through web chats
When single parent is too an option
Surely this day demands huge celebration.

Miss Universe Sushmita Sen. adopted a girl child
Set example to be single parent for a daughter
Just few months back young boy of 28 adopted a baby boy with special needs
Parenting needs spring of love
Foster or biological
Unconditional love and care plays the role magical.

Someone who smilingly hugs
Someone who stands in support even if the child is blind, deaf or dumb
Someone who toils day and night to bring luxuries of life
Someone who inspires for success
Someone who accepts your failure too
Not essentially only biological
But the bond is more powerful
Global Parents Day many celebrated and well spent
Some visited the Old Age homes
Rendering service hours in taking care of old inmates
Ironical it was
Those whom they bred as parents they left them there
Those who were deprived of hopeful hand throughout childhood
They found tears from wrinkled eyes after their hug
More precious than solitaires bagful
Both the sides saw reflection of divinity in the embrace.

Brother Sister Bond

She yelled at him,
"You are a bad boy
I will tell papa you hid my toy."

He shouted in return,
"O little naughty girl!
You disturbed me and spoiled my game too.
I will tell Mom about you."

This is the way,
In each other's company,
while playing indoors lido or carom
while in the game outdoors cricket or chasing or hide and seek
they giggle together and they fight with each other.
They compete to get parent's compliment.

She takes care of her brother's valuables all time.
He is younger or older,
for her he is the bravest soldier.
For him she is the caretaker sweetest.
Once they reach the age of maturity
They keep some time for each other on priority.

Every other day is Mother's Day.

In the summer afternoon heat
I saw a cute chubby boy coaxing mother for the treat!!
Mom was looking with meaningful eyes
towards a lady in Lemon floral suit
Lovely was the scene
Lovely were the expressions!!
Two generations celebrating the same day!!
They entered Bikanerwala
My curious eyes followed the trio towards the stairs.
A handsome person in mid twenties was escorting two women.
From face cut resemblance the woman on his right was his mom
Diva draped in denim Capri and baby pink kurti,
With prominent baby bump was his child's mother to be.
Her mysterious smile reminded me Monalisa!
I drowned in the memories of my own time!!
How magical moments are those when kicks in womb communicate a lot.
With moist eyes and smiling lips
I looked at the picture of my mom
I realize her absence
I recall the fabulous moments we shared
From my birth till I attained motherhood
That soft spoken soft skinned soft cushion of my life had been my mom.
Every other day for me is Mother's Day.Top of Form

Ode to Fathers

For centuries altogether
Fathers were subjected to a big torture
Tender by heart but they had to carry stern look as signature
The social practices deprived them the charm of cuddling the offspring
Blood of his own blood
Even Shakespeare described fathers made of different mettle
Someone who keeps working for his children till they settle

Before the dawn of twenty first century
Fathers were forced to wear big moustache matching with frown
Now the concepts have totally changed
Each man is Cool Daddy indeed
Those who marry they keep friendly terms with children
Those who remain single
They adopt the bundles of love deserted by parents

Valiant fathers are the ex servicemen
Willfully they allow their kin to join the most dangerous profession
Bravest fathers are those few too
Who accept and support LGBT sons or daughters too
Toughest fathers show the way
But never spread soft cushions for successful walkway.

No doubt
To see this beautiful side of personality
Parents wait to tie their sons in the bonds of matrimony.

June 19, 2016

Ode to Childhood

Chubby cheeks
First looking at a toy
Expressions coy
Within moments toy dismantled
In the cushion of chubby cheeks is hidden a geek!!!!
Anger and Smile
Catch attention of grownups from a mile!!!!
Toffees Chocolates
Ice cream and Cakes
Are marketed for their sake
Child is the father of man"
Once wrote William Wordsworth
Actually he was true then and even today
Children today are smarter
Elders feel in tongue tarter
T.V. promotions are for their wish list a starter
Gone are the days of innocence
Child of Net age knows branded fragrance!!!!
Children in a family just one or two
Enjoy Children's Day daily too!!!!
In the new era Children's Day
must mean to keep alive the Child within you!!!
Carefree and Caring
Hurried and Healthy
Inquisitive and Intelligent
Loving and Loyal
Dodgy and Determent
Childhood is the best age
Easy it is then to move ahead crisscrossing the lives maze.

November 14, 2012

Ode to Doctors

White coat and stethoscope around the neck
The dress code for them
From the neighborhood clinic to super specialty hospital
From rural India to high end London
Life is not easy, rosy and livable without them
Before you are born
An Obstetrician and Gynecologist take pre natal care
Then post birth you are observed periodically by a Pediatrician
Infancy is safe for they are there to monitor your growth
You get teeth then enter in your life a Dentist
The growing up confusions in adolescence are skillfully handled by
Psychologist
Your beauty urge is satiated by kind cruelty of Cosmetic Surgeon's knife
In Hollywood and Bollywood many find God in Cosmetologist
Life style endangers your internal system
Do not worry
There is battery of specialist to heal or repair your system
From head to toe
Orthopedics understands your bones and joints
Physiotherapist helps your mobility post any surgery
Dietician tells you what to eat
Cardiologist keeps your heart safe
Neurologist knows how to treat your nerves and brain
Then there is General Physician
Sort of family health problem encyclopedia
But these days their number is reducing
For each body part a separate specialist is consulted for treating
For vision consult an Ophthalmologist
For skin care there is Dermatologist
There are also Speech Therapists

You die at home or in hospital
You are alive till the Death certificate is signed by a Doctor
Now you know that from Conception to the last breathe
God remains with you in the guise of two
Natural caretaker and healer your mother
Second one is your Doctor
The one who studies allopathic system is Allopath
The one who uses nature for cure is Naturopath
The one prescribing sweet tablets dipped in liquids is Homeopath
The one using ancient medicine system ayurveda is Vaidya
The one practicing unani system is called Hakeem

Nomenclature may call them by any name
Doctors can only to our diseases tame.

July 01, 2016 at 10 am

Let's start celebrating ageing.

Enjoying thrill till count of thirty nine
Stepping a foot in the forty
Earlier all thought only for men it permitted to be naughty.
In this new millennia
People when foraying forty feel celebration mania.
Men and women in their joints may feel knotty
they continue being bubbly though walking wonky.
They too are proud to be plus forty!
It is in 21century their time to be seen in this age as hot!
Many cosmetic brands in their advertisements
keep for this ever-young breed a slot!
Children grown up
it's the time for real fun
Enjoyment of life for forty plus has just begun.
Shakespeare called it middle age
for fast friend "BUDAPA" it sets stage.
Infancy lasted eighteen months.
Childhood spanned the next ten years.
Adolescence was short-lived transition.
Teenage was full of confusion.
Youth started in twentieth year.
In forties Youth is in the last gear.
People play and enjoy
A man in forties thinks himself still a boy
Women are no less.
They also take them to be young lass!
Frantic shopping of sunscreens
Men women dye hair to look evergreen
Many among them step ahead to lead
wisely in pension fund they invest indeed.
For good health figure and vigor
Spend time on themselves being regular
Forget eighteen century caging
let's start celebrating ageing.

To Men on Their Day

The day dedicated to Men all over the world
It is being celebrated today.
Though each day is everywhere their day!
Father, Brother, Husband, Son and Friend
Wishing them especially this day is the latest trend!
The day is meant to salute the Man missing in many.
The Man is the one who-

> Has kind heart that cares for all.
> Has strength to protect the others selflessly.
> Has the essence of mannerism.

The Man these days has become –

- Showcase partner in matrimony.
- Credit filler in the plastic money of his younglings.
- Target achiever employee in the office.
- Jigsaw puzzle on his own identity.

The day is meant to salute The Man missing in many.

Valor & Patriotism

Soldiers

Sometimes I think
in war time what do soldiers drink!!
Do they get the time to sleep!!
Has God given them any special stomach!!
Amid those trees
those hidden enemies,
How do they satiate their urge to eat potato fries!!

When mother in me doesn't eat a morsel
lest my child eats so!!
O Soldier how difficult is for your mom eating a morsel too!!

While walking when talking
I reach the edge
I get scared to step even an inch!!
Then I think O Soldier you embrace dare devilry with wink
you make the enemy to depth sink!
Sometimes I think
what do the soldiers in war time do think!!
There came the answer from within!!
Soldiers do not think
they act on their instinct!!
If they will not!!
Then instead of enemy
in their battalion will be dead and injured many!!!
Soldiers act and do fast think
we sleep at night
their eyes even not allowed winning!!!
My head and heart fills with gratitude
whenever about Soldiers I do think.

Just last night

With God I indulged in an argument forthright
To pacify myself and to know
And asked these questions in a row
"O Almighty Thou art the creator of this planet
Tell me then the formulae used in making Indian Army combatant."
He just smiled and kept quiet
Rather He patted his soft hand on my head very light
"O Lord of Power have you added some extra input in these fighter?"
Amused at my innocent query
Started He blinked his eyes beaming merry
"It is true my child
These warriors who spend their youth in wild
They do have extra amount of Determination
They are designed to serve selflessly their nation."

"Under Thou lotus feet I do have the reliance
So you mean Soldiers in each country are created for public defense.
But then why you created the mercenaries?
Are they also given some extra energy?"

The Divine Aura of Almighty grew more
He flew my soul towards Sopore
There He made me observe and understand
The Negative and Positive energy imbalance created in mind

The thunder in the sky
Early in the morning compelled me to open the eyes.
Except for the limited traces of our conversation
Almighty Lord cleverly pressed on other part deletion
The beauty of grey clouds and rain
Made me think of possible flood in Kashmir Valley again

Besides ensuring safety at borders
These brave combatants help carry safely expectant mothers
In crisis of any type
Without creating about it any hype.
Earthquake may shake the buildings but not their resolution
Landslide, bomb blasts, tsunami the soldiers report for rescue mission

Away from families they live life of saint
They are special souls for our safety on Earth descent.

July 18, 2016, 7:35 pm

Diwali at Line of Control

Small earthen lamps lighted.
Hope in many hearts ignited.
When near the fence our soldiers lit the candles,
From across Line of Control the bullets get fired as hurdle.
Short split second of silence,
then there is roar of exchanging fires.
We know across the country
Indian armed forces get full support and respect.
This is something our enemy can never digest.
They lure some misguided minds.
They are used by the enemy in setting up land mines.
Perhaps our soldiers at boarder have chest broader.
They use grenades just like crackers!!
For them every day is Diwali!!
Dhoom Dhoom Dhadaam!!
The bombs they blast! They keep the Tricolor flying pole steadfast!
Away from mom, dad, brother, sister
Away from darling spouse and children!
They, the sons of soil, let their body toil.
The nefarious designs of enemy they do foil.
They, the sons of soil, play daily deadly Diwali with each ceasefire violations.
They assure us Indians enjoy safe feisty festive celebrations.

‖ *Points to ponder*

I was sitting on my soft cushioned couch.
The television was switched on.
At 11 a.m.
Watching the news bulletin
I become an eyewitness.
The channels airing
"26/11 repeat at Kenya."
The bullets!
The people trying to take refuge!
Life at gun point proves,
"Praying to the mercenaries no use."
Humanity for them is no good excuse.
Just then echoes in my grey matter
the words from a soldier's letter
"In Kashmir somewhere
I had to encounter
few infiltrators
as per rule our target was Wasim only.
His family was not our enemy.
Wearing combat attire,
with arsenal,
we knocked the door.
Out came a burqa clad female.
Her eyes made me feel in her my mother in an instant there.
My gaze touched her feet.
She too had blessed me indeed!
Her eyes carried the pain.
The same pain I saw each time I left my home when duty bound!
A conflict arose within

"Am I doing right?
"Am I taking her son?
Moist eyes
Moist mind
I followed the call of duty".
Now I ponder
Soldiers saving hostages
are they going through some conflict of duty and heart too?

It is Patriotism in a Way

In a nation as unique as my motherland,
Adding people from diverse ethnic backgrounds as Face book friend.
It is Patriotism in a way!!
Playing pranks with car pool friends,
Relishing on diverse cuisines,
 and standing guard against terrorism.
It is Patriotism in a way!!
People pay timely the taxes of all hues.
Common men clear all water and electricity dues.
It is Patriotism in a way!!
Players play as individual or team game.
Work for winning it for sake of nation's name.
It is Patriotism in a way!!
Majority of the motorists abide by road signage.
With intra country migration,
People learn diverse languages!!
It is Patriotism in a way!!
Some selflessly work for the welfare of others.
Others establish business to employ many youngsters.
It is Patriotism in a way!!
Poets, Journo, Writers and Scientists
Utilize wits, wisdom and words positively do their best.
It is Patriotism in a way!!

25/01/2015 9:58pm

Sportsman spirit takes A Back Seat!

Whenever big bro India
plays against young one Pakistan
Sportsmanship takes a back seat.
Sparrows forget to tweet!!!
Hens hold eggs within!!!!
Barber may cut half beard or moustache!!!
Whether school or office
Every where you can find
Curious non cricket lover too asking
"What is the score?"
It is the question to be answered more and more.
The game may be any.
The level may be any.
Cricket, Kabaddi, Football or Hockey
Fans do not accept big bro's defeat!
At night or day the win results in treat!
Its not me but Ranbir and Rishi Kapoor in commercials say
"T20 is neither played or viewed in a gentleman's way"
We can treat the rarest disease of any Pakistani the best way
we can let Kasab and Abu Fazal bloat
eating biryani in our jails
but sportsman spirit in the field of game takes a back seat
It takes a backseat!
It takes a back seat!

October 01, 2012

Comparison & Description

Book vs. E Book

There were many on the study table.
Bonded and Colorful
Thin and Voluminous,
Pages glossy or crimson crinkled.
Just then their attention was caught.
They heard, "How are you oldies?"
With frown within the group the books looked for the speaker.
Finally they found the one who jibed at them.
A reader had just logged on the desktop.
He had opened a site to find new poem to recite.
The E Book was the teaser.
This flexible enchanter,
the new creation by Humans,
The baby of e- technology reflected the attitude!
"Born out of us
she reflects attitude in place of gratitude!"
They all together,
knew it well;
this new incarnation of Knowledge would have the boom.
They then addressed her "Dear youngster be humble.
For you do not know someone may outshine even you some day.
Your popularity depends on our beauty anyway."
Mutely the exchange was going on
until the Books on study table were open
and the E Book was logged on.

Love Vs Lust

Lust is selfish
Love is selfless
Lust chases
Loves rests
Lust leads to obsession
Love leads to salvation
Lust leads to sulking
Love leads to caring
Lust surfaces in open
Love pearl stays in oyster hidden
Lust looses interest when bed ridden
Love keeps the warmth around till the last
Lust satisfies high hormones
Love establishes bonds even with life around under ozone.

Love and Hate

They do co exist in mind
Love is blind
Hate is unkind
Love knows no reason
Hate leaves no reason
Love is powerful
Wins over the enemies
Hate often leads to self injuries
Love leads to passion
Hate ignites burning sensation
Love soothes smoothens life
Hate sulks brings in bulk strife
Love is often at first sight
Hate emerges at first fight

Words vs. Silence

Words reveal you
Silence conceals you

Words carry music
Silence makes mystic

Words may start a fight
Silence allows insight

Words compliment eyes
Silence communicate using eyes

Words paint a picture
Silence reads the picture

Words float in air
Silence makes feel the air

Words are gift of gab
Silence lets Spirituality grab

Words reflect inspection
Silence is introspection

Words for some are play station
Silence for wise is meditation

Words cheer
Silence spells the fear

Marriage or Mirage

Marriage and mirage are no different
Both confuse eyes
Watching newlyweds tempts many
To look extra beautiful
Spending bags of money
On skin polishing
Figure correction
Amazing dress collection
Bride hogs limelight
Groom gets sidelined
Just like mirage
Only those who have tied the knot can tell
One moment it is heaven the next a hell
Mirage is full of mystery
For newly married Shivani life is like pastry
Full of aroma and garnished with cherry
She is enjoying life with her Prince Harry
Both of them keep
Relatives friends waiting
To get the confirmed breakfast lunch or dinner invites
Their hosts are ready to each other fight
Poor couple they hardly get any sleep at night
For the ruffian mosquitoes in their own merriment to them they bite
So she understood
Marriage is mirage

Pleasure vs. Happiness

Moralist lived centuries ago
Her smile made her painter immortal
Researchers have sleepless nights
Even on the costliest and the most pleasurable bed
Their happiness lies in cracking the mystery of her smile.
Dubai or suburban chawl in Mumbai
Wealthiest Sheikh or penniless Farookh
Both are unhappy
Both are restless
When disease snatches away their dearest
Pleasure is momentary
New acquisition
New dress
New address
New musical instrument
Addition expansion of business empire
All are to measure
How much money can get you pleasure?
Mother Teresa's smile is treasure
From such smile Happiness is measure
Hold the hand let someone cross the road
Listen patiently for redressed
Give share to a hungry from your bite
A pat of reassurance
Brings solace and smile
Alexander the great
Told his men
To let his empty palms hang out of his coffin
Be shown
To those who moan

"With power and money
pleasures enjoyed unmeasured.
Palms emptiness yells
there was no happiness."
Satisfaction Solace never to money embrace
in serving humanity
Happiness you trace.
Pleasure is short lived
Happiness in spiritual acts engraved.

Mars vs. Venus in Delhi Metro

Pink line envoy many
either it is a station
At Yellow, Blue or Red metro line in Delhi.
Across the line are
Dainty damsels all decked up
Wearing attires as diverse as our nation
from floral chiffon saris
to trendy tees with aperies
Though draped in burqa few
Intricate design of embroidery on burqa mesmerizes too
Some are tall some are short
From curly to silky straight hair
Till shoulder or waist length
Let loose or tied in a bun or equally beautiful clutches holding then
together
Some in groups chatting
Some with plugged in earphones enjoying music
Few are quiet observers
Glancing on different style
Hand bags and flat to high heel footwear
Across the Pink line
The scene is all together different
Wearing striped check or plain shirts
Boys are trying a queue to maintain
These creatures from Mars
Are within themselves at war
They are even differently dressed
But on their faces it shows they are stressed

Some are carrying laptop bags on shoulder
Others are carrying a sleek handbag
Some are bearded Some clean shaven
Few try to show their biceps and tattoos
Some are supporting different moustaches
Sikh boys wearing matching Turban
Men are in even long kurta pajamas

When Metro halts
Doors open
From Pink bogies
Neatly dressed
Fully relaxed
Chirping beauties come out
Other enter equally cool
But men it seems
Need to put no self effort in alighting
A wave pushes them out
The greater push to be inside to
The eyes to eyes war
Across the Pink privileges
And these Mars population is classic
From here they focus on chicks
There the serenity smiles at them
Enjoy Delhi Metro
What Mars vs. Venus means
You will come to know

Ode to Dhabas on Indian National Highways

Truckers and Travelers
Some young revelers
Love to zip fast
Fields with crops left past

Regular riders on the highway
Halt at their favorite eateries for the brief stay.
They park the vehicles and recharge their phones too
Pay decent amount for the food they chew.

Loud music and table chairs lay in open
Full size advertisement banners of sponsors.
Catch the attention of hungry souls,
Just two kilometers before the next township
Truckers, Roadways buses, cars, and bikers have their different goals.

Whenever, a car towards the compound reaches,
a male attendant with duster in his hand rushes.
He swiftly wipes the car windscreen.
Within minute appears the other attendant on the scene.
Just like breathless Shankar Raghvan
He reads the menu for free to be heard by everyone.
"Sir welcome to our dhabha by me.
What would you like to have? Please tell me.
For you we have tea, coffee, lassi, shikanji and cold drink.
We are famous for mouth watering Aloo prantha,
Gobi prantha,
Paneer prantha,
Amritsari daal with naan."
In between, the man at cash counters shouts, at the waiter,
"Oye Chhotu you clean the table and chair.
Carefully note down their food order."

Third one guides in soft sweeter tone,
"Yes madam ...washroom facility that side
And cute baby just chill on swings the other side."

All tables gradually get occupied
those who are still to be served the order
on others' table their eyes keep spying.
Customers watch the man carrying tray.
Eyes of those waiting follow his way.
At tandoor the chef's hands clap
after each prantha he pastes
inside oven in haste.
Air is filled with aroma
And
In rains besides mud
Space is brimming with flies too!

Since they drive for long
Instead of table chair
Truckers prefer dhaba
To lay on choir charpoy
Sipping loud their chai

Some dhabas are known for special dishes
Foodies to satiate taste buds
Reach there with endless wishes
On Indian highways
Dhabas pray for hungry traveler always.

August 04, 2012, 04:27 p.m.

Gym has undergone makeover

Replacing the heavy grinding stone
Mechanized gadgets help maintain skin tone
This place is vibrant with activity
Girls and boys work out in well ventilated vicinity.
Some put efforts to fight obesity.
Some others busy boosting their immunity
Surely all keep their trainers on mobility
Cycling, Jumping, Pushups
make the blood in vessels to pump.
It benefits both skinny and plump.
Crunches, Pilates, Abs training
All aid in flexibility and strength building.
Leg presses, Chest presses, Leg curls, Arm curls and Rowing
Are pepped up with music listening.
Some sweat a lot
Some chew the gum a lot
Some on treadmill walk lost in thought
Some burn calories to relax
Others are unable to forget the office stress
Gyms normally have spacious floors
with transparent doors
Those who love gym
For them Yoga is slower in rhythm

Library: Myths are set ablaze here.

Library is the place where
Myths are set ablaze
Wisdom of the world stacked neatly
Books of all sizes
On all possible topics
Hard bound Soft bound
Even some special editions
Annual Monthly Fortnightly
Daily arrivals
Systematically stamped stocked in shelves
With book in hand readers are lost in themselves
Though CD versions are also there
But reading the words that do not run
Its still great fun
Books are so revered
that only Silence is preferred
To taste the world of facts fantasy fiction
well lit well organized room gives satisfaction
It's here you realize.
Besides the title, author and publisher
A book's identity is its accession number.
Library
it has become boundless and boundary less
It has entered the electronic era
To taste the flavor of your choice
In e-library you enjoy reading without noise
You can drift in the world of visualization
Simply plug the earphones and play the audio version
Kindle and You tube are mini libraries virtually
you search a book in both

Using catalogue
A continuous dialogue goes on within
E library makes you miss the dust
And those yellow crinkled pages
A significant feature that tells the book has been on shelf for ages.
E or real world building
It is a fact strange that
Library is the place where
Myths are set ablaze

30 June 2012

Faith, Philosophy & Contemporary

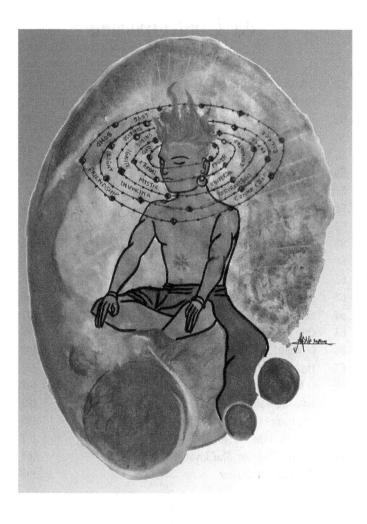

Ode to Lord Shiva

Unique Mystic
Always busy focusing world too wide within!
He does not say that
rather to the mortals he does show
Smearing on forehead the ash from crematorium
Body is mortal but he is IMMORTAL!
He lets snake wriggle around his neck
He wears Lion skin
He sits with one arm resting on his Trishul!
He hardly joins the erstwhile ranks of Inderlok in witnessing Rambha or Maneka.
They drink Somras but he knows the art of digesting Snake venom!
Unique Mystic
Always busy focusing world too wide within!
He proves to us
be firm and do not feel alone.
Nature gives you company
Trees, Doves, River Ganga, Moon, Bull Nandy are more than many!
Unique Mystic
Always busy focusing world too wide within!
Happy he is in his simplicity!
Most suitable Bachelor he had been for Sati and later for Parvati!
He dances well.
He acts well.
He dives deep within to explore truth.
No one else but he has that ire to lit Fire using the rays from eyes!
Only He can be sitting cool atop icy Himalayan hill top.

March 10, 2013

On Buddha's Salvation Day

If you want Peace
Go under the shade of Bhodhi tree.
If you want Peace
Then Close eyes towards Worldly temptations please.
If you want Peace
Then close eyes and find Solace within.
If you want Peace
Then be surrounded by serene Nature.
When you get Peace
Just like Gautama Buddha you will be at Peace.
He left the lavish life.
He left the worldly bonds.
He stopped belonging to himself.
He belongs to all in the world forever.
☺ ☺ ☺ ☺ ☺
All celebrate his Salvation Day today.

Success Too Is Time Bound!!

Gazing at life around
some amazing truth I found
Growth is time bound!!!
Success too is time bound!!!
Daily my curious eyes watch the buds in flower beds
Gardner timely does all that needed
But its only the destined time that bud opens
Petal by petal
Beauty unfolds
With it unfolds the Success!!!
Sweat of gardener is the dew shining on pink petals
Chrysanthemum wins accolades!!!
His efforts rewarded!!!
Air is sensed not seen
Success to is sensed not seen!!!
Life in a seed is hidden
Noticed only when it sprouts!!!
Life is breathing within
but it's counted only when born!!!
Efforts are the Air
Result is Success!!!
Success is as colorful as rainbow!!!
For an actor it's in award winning role
For a doctor it's in every life secured
For a chef it's in the taste of the dish
For a tailor its in the costume's best finish
For a learner it's in the lesson learnt
For a philanthropist it's in charity
For a teacher it's in concept clarity!!!

Unsolved Mystery

Again a fact from pages of history
Pinpointed at unsolved mystery
Mythology says we all are with five elements made
But rubbing Flintstones if by chance was Fire created
so it means earlier with only four we were generated!!!
If we survive and grow in coffin like womb
then why are we laid post death in a tomb?
Who created us all and all the Cosmos??
Where is hidden that Super efficient Super boss??
Amoeba Paramecium all can themselves reproduce
then why surplus internal external organs in any factory not produce???
Born pure and fearless
why we find life steer less?
Those who get Enlightened
Why they could not fully share
for all these queries the search within is there

June 14, 2012, 3:38 p.m.

Have you ever thought?

Whenever we wish to convey a trait
we use Simile
we love to say someone is:
as loyal as dog
as cunning as fox
as swift as bee
as kind as tree
as brave as tiger
as dark as raven
as slow as sloth
as big as elephant
as chirpy as bird
as hard working as an ass.
Have you ever thought why we humans compare a lot?
Do we have some original trait or not?
Ever other living creatures
Envy our features?
To fly high why we have no feathers?

Some Similarities

When I looked up in the sky
Stray clouds were floating by
Just then my grey matter got in action
Between Thoughts and Clouds
there is similarity by fraction!
Both are can't be taught
Both carry the weight
Both are the carriers

When I inhaled the fragrant air
Mulberry tree near my gate caught my attention then and there
Those red ripe mulberries added the sweet fragrance
Some similarities got highlighted by chance!
Between Fragrance and Fame
Both are associated with name,
both reach others, the owner need not to bother.

When I entered my kitchen
my daughter gave her wish list then!!!
Brain pondered again
Wishes and Sea Waves seemed similar now!!!
Both are endless!!
Both are short lived.
Both keep on changing!

April 12, 2013, 7:59 p.m.

Decoding Telepathy

Just at 11: 15 am by the clock flashed a desire in my heart!
How to send the packet of my ink's imprint to my dear Mamaji!
Before I could think of the options
My phone bell rang
Screen displayed the caller identity.
"Mama"
OMG! My desire reached his heart so fast!
His affectionate voice expressed the same
That was running in my brain!

We both live in two different states.
But still the invisible waves they connected us so fast!

Is it the genetic connect that made it possible?
Is it the work of invisible unbelievable good souls?
Do such souls carry the vibes?
Do our thoughts emit in air some high frequency waves?

Just not only with me
This happens in the lives of many.
Some call it "Coincidence"
Some address it as "Intuition"
Some scholars call it "Telepathy"
Many are still trying to decode these vibes.

May 22, 2016, 12 pm

Controversy: Creativity's Ugly baby

It is Creativity's ugly baby.
It divides the people in different lobby.
It is born on bed of curiosity.
It travels at irregular velocity.
It erupts where there is more diversity.
It is friend of fire.
It follows even to the pyre.
It is Universal patent.
It makes people lament later.
It keeps issues burning.
It uses mischief in mind to keep going.
It makes paparazzi' have good earning.

June 29, 2012, 7: 05 pm

Crisis is the best friend

It makes you cool
It gives you a tool
It makes you cry
It makes you try
Crisis is your best friend
It brings to surface reality
Of men and mentality
It makes you know
Of how you are hit with bow
Crisis is your best friend
It leaves you richer
It is the best teacher
It brings in open hidden friends
It showcases openly their bonds
Crisis is the best friend
Crisis is the best friend

A Little Gesture but a Big Relief

Ever you thought why toothless smiles are so infectious?
Either new born babies are toothless
or
those aged living second childhood are toothless.
An infant does not discriminates in passing smile
An old too does not differentiates in showering affection through smile
A little gesture is the smile indeed!
It is gesture of love
It is gesture of happiness
It is gesture of content soul within.
Ever you wondered such small an effort brings
Big relief
Bridges the gap
Bounces back cheer on a sad face.
Besides smile listening embalms someone in pain
At times no medicine works better but a human ear
At times no reciprocation is needed but a mute companion
At times no money is required but just a careful presence of dear ones
Smilingly the soft touch of hand
its all they need to heal the wound
its all they need to lighten the burden of load
A timely expressed repentance
A timely extended helping hand
A timely accepted the extended hand
A timely intervention amid a fight
All these are small gestures that bring a big relief indeed.

October 23, 2015, 11:22 am

The Load Of Expectations

"Are you expecting?"
This brings in a shy naughty smile on her face.
With this starts the journey of Expectations!!
The world around makes the Expectant mother cautious.
"Wow! Do you get great desire for some special food?"
"You got the baby kick?"
She realizes the onset of a new bond.
The bond that is unique.
The bond that is so private.
She starts getting troubled with load of Expectations.
Suggestions pour for free from all
she gets guided on:
The food she must eat,
the pictures she must see,
the words to speak and
the books to read.
Before coming to taste the life outside
in small placenta inside
to be born human
starts taking care of Expectations!!
Periodic visits to the doctor
Confirms the growth on scale of medical expectations!!
Though birth and death are in hands of God
Expected date of birth is still declared!!
"Congrats!!"
With these words the river of Expectations changes it course
"Are the booster doses given as scheduled?"
With growth of the child
Expectations go wild

Then it reaches a time frame
When anxiety over takes in game.
The soul gets trapped in vicious circle
Just like a crazy musk deer trying to reach the fragrance spins in circle
The school
The college
The campus selection
The search for life partners
And then expectation of grand children

We keep carrying this load of Expectation.

7 July 2015

Stigma

No disagreement with the fact
A black dot on big white paper catches the eye attention instant
But the paper does hold no regret
It knows
Neither the dot is eternal
Nor is the life of the white paper.
But the same is not the psyche of us humans.
Stigma is the unbearable dot on integrity
Silently violently it kills dignity
Though we are sure
Death buries and burns the body and name
And still brain starts sulking
Sinking in the whirlpool of thoughts
When the dubious statements reach the ears
Post doing many rounds in the tiny world of friends and foes around.

Murderous weapon it's for centuries at large
In the name of honor capability self esteem it splurges
Stigma grips slowly firmly like boa constrictor
Skin color
Gender
Salary
Reasons to torture are many
Weakened by unrealistic pressure
Victims of it forget to live in pleasure
they deprive themselves of Nature's beautiful treasure

Spiritual discourses and Divine intervention
At times help in saving the suffering population.

Ode to Silence

Silence embarks the journey of life!
Silence shuts the doors on embers of life!
Silence allows the eyes communicate.
Silence enhances listening.
Silence creates Suspense.
Silence is the best offense.
Silence is the best defense.
Silence of friend annoys.
Silence of enemies soothes.
Silence closes doors of disturbance.
Silence opens gates of meeting the Self within.
Silence is essential for inward inspection.
Silence with eyes closed is meditation.
Silence while in sleep is natural relaxation.
Silence signifies worth of words.

Nov 22, 2013, 10:21 pm

Ode to Words

Words are like birds.
They keep flying.
Words are like sweet.
They keep sticking.
Words are like chewing gum.
They need biting.
Words are like dress.
They keep changing.
Words are like sword.
They keep slashing.
Words are like museum.
They keep accumulating.
Words are like mirror.
They keep truthfully reflecting.
Words are like river.
They keep ideas flowing.
Words are like ornament.
They keep beautifying.

June 23, 2012

Ode to Smile

When saliva drooling rosy lips and twinkling eyes
Create cute curve on chubby cheeks
The smile that appears is mesmerizing.
It pulls people like a magnet.
Caste, color, creed are all forgotten.
All just wish to cuddle the Cherub!

The teen age smile carries mystery.
Manner, time, purpose and place add variety.
Some smile to please.
Some smile to tease.
Some smile to accept
some smile to hide hurt
some smile enchants opposites
Mr. as well as Ms. beautiful smile are announced on stage.
Titles are chased in this age.

Smile on wrinkled face capsizes too!
Cheeks within and teeth missing
Some look so cute when grinning.
Some smile to hide their grief.
Some smile as sign of relief.

Smile of a teacher is an assurance of affection and belief.
Smile of a learner is
blend of ignorance, innocence and mischief.

Smile of an air crew is an advertisement.
Smile of a nurse conveys, "It won't pain."
Smile of a patient conveys, "Handle me with care please!"

Smile is undoubtedly a lip curve.
It is the strongest weapon too!
Try it on the enemy.
See your smile hits the most!
Smile is a natural gift.
It bridges the rift.
So I say
Smile! Smile! Smile!
Just forget worldly your pain.
Smile! Smile! Smile!

O Night! You are so great!

You are synonymous with hopelessness.
You are the darkness.
In your depth lies the struggle of the day
You try your level best to keep energy enthusiasm at your bay.
You are the savior most misunderstood.
You conserve success.
You conceal it in your darkness.
Unknown unexpected unborn joy hood
O Night! You are so great!
You allow the dreams to destiny create
O Night! You are so great!
You are so great!

June 3, 2012, 12:04 am

Have you ever noticed Wait?

Have you ever noticed who waits the most?
The Sun in the morning to rise
Or
the Moon in the evening to rise

Have you ever understood who waits the best?
A farmer who toils day and night for others' delight
Or
a soldier who guards a post selflessly though sleep deprived.

Have you ever acknowledged who waits the least?
A wave of human desire
Or
a rumor to spread like fire

Have you ever noticed who waits the cutest?
An infant with a bib looking at mom
Or
an unborn dream growing in womb of to be mom

Have you ever observed who waits the shortest?
A pair of eyes to wink
Or
A pair of lips to smile

June 7, 2012, 12:22 pm

O Memories! Thou art immortal!

Moments enjoyed
Moments lived
Part of growing
Its aroma brewing
Sometimes it amazes
Why the time not freezes
Memories
They remain hidden
In reunions they enliven
They hold all together
Sweet and sour taste of life altogether
Memories
They bind like glue
Tears flow without any clue
They strengthen their hold
They are more treasure able than gold
Memories
Reflect in old collections
Of photos, relics, mementoes and coins
O Memories! You are immortal!

June 01, 2012, 11:13 am

Looking Good Syndrome!

Watching the mythical show Devon ke dev Mahadev
The anger of Ma Parvati on Lord Shiva
To reflect her annoyance at not getting the garland
Before the scene could move to the next frame
Katrina Kaif promoting Veet for smooth hair free skin popped up!
As if single advertisement was not suffice
Shah Rukh emerged to lure men for fairer skin tone
Baba Ramdev also could not be stopped
Yoga Day seems his brand.
Thank the two minutes commercial break got over
Lord Shiva with his consort Ma Parvati again appeared
Now the reason of annoyance got clear
The flowers in the garland He brought were withered.
OMG! So Ma Parvati too was bugged with looking beautiful syndrome!
This bug has survived so many millenniums
This bug could create the rift among Gods
Then how humans can be spared?

World economies thrive on this syndrome
Eternal beauty remains skin deep
But in 2016 it surfaced on ramp
In a bid to revive its significance
First it was in city named Ludhiana
Acid attack victim walked in tandem on the ramp
Her gracious attire and confident cat walk
Made many in awe to get a chance to talk

Reshma Qureshi went a step further
Puzzled the world with beauty of her inner strength
Walked with other divas
Her smile on the scared face
Made her win the race

She created new history
Her beauty visible earlier caught her in the tangles of ire
Her beauty she showcased now earned her many admires.

But beauty syndrome bugs many.

September 16, 2016, 8:12 pm

Hindrances Are the Best Buddies

When we look back in the life
The pain of the struggle and strife
We feel like thanking hindrances
The sweetness of sweat is in taking chances

If there were no obstacles on the way
Could we enjoy the flame of fame for a day?

Usain Bolt or Phelp look at the hurdles they do face
One while swimming and other in the race
Dipa Karmaker took the risk of performing Prod nova

A small trek passage
Blocked the possibility of saving life of his wife
Hindrance inspired Dasrath Manjhi
He single handed challenged the mountain
With his dogged determination
At his pace he carved a motor able road
Winner he stood in creating history.

Away from the prying eyes
Devoting the time after work hours
Just to inspire the sleepy world around
Nek Chand Sharma spent years
Converting waste products and land
To tourist attraction in Chandigarh

Jadav Molai Payeng of Assam
Sensed the importance of snakes in eco system
A simple forest laborer put life back in land
Within years lush green forest he revived
On the fame and prizes he was not eyeing.

Stephen Hawkins, Sudha Chandran, Tenny Grey- Thopson
Their disabilities for the world were hindrances
But the greater will power to win over
These titanium willed left nothing to chances.

When we look around in Nature
Where ever the hindrances have been tapped
The dams got created
The gift of hydro power generation tasted

Nature too says
Hindrances are our best buddies anyway.

September 13, 2016, 7:43 pm

Life Goes On Forever!

The world was in shock
When it was 9/11 in New York
The world was again in shock
When 9/11 dawned in 2016 at 12 'o' clock

Media got jitters
When ballot in USA favored Trump and Hillary worthless
Hoarders got shivers
When Modi declared high denomination currency invalid and useless
9/11 brought down tall Twin Towers
Pentagon too suffered some attacks
9/11/2016 down scaled the pride in wallets of many
Average Indian got busy in counting and collecting money
Media used the disaster bites to boost TRP
Media used the chaos confusion bites to boost TRP
Twin Towers crash instilled anger and fear
1000 and 500 INR demise today caused anger and fear

Life did not stop then
Life has not stopped today
Life goes on forever
Currencies and Leaders cease to exist forever.
With passage of time the wounds of loss do heal
With passage of time wallets too get filled.

November 9, 2016, 7: 47 pm

Neither 'He' nor 'She' lovable acceptable 'Ze'

Learning the alphabets of true Equality
Oxford University lead by introducing 'Ze'
When next time you meet Arthur or Amit or Aslam
When next time you greet Alice or Aruna or Afsana
While sharing your interaction with any
You just need to use 'Ze' eliminating their gender identity
God only knows, whom He created with penis but the psyche feminine.
God only knows, whom He created with vagina but the burning fire within masculine.
Though the Creator never with wisdom attached body basics
but for centuries those born as Transgender suffered in the garb of ethics.
Happy the dusk of 2016 is bringing brighter dawn in 2017.

December 12, 2016, 3:10 p.m.

War against Cancer

Temptation, Peer persuasion are big traps.
The first try leads to big cry.
I am not here for teaching tips or preaching.
If this summoning could save my father
I had summoned him many times.
If fitness regime alone could save cricketer Yuvraj
He coughed blood when he played the Winning World Cup.
He recovered the cancer when the medication routine forced food modification.

Was eating right food a difficult choice earlier?
Was taking care of good sleep a big hurdle?

To please others
Puffing the butts on butts
Does not make anyone Hero
Gobbling the mouthful of junk food
Builds gradually the Cancer Castle

To those who tempted you
Do not suffer your pain and loss
They who paint a fantasy of thrills
They never accompany you for Chemo drill

The heat produced as effect of Chemo Therapy
Takes away the charm and beauty physically

Time to stop cursing the pollution and pesticides
After all it is the result of your weak resolution and fake pride.

Companies are at fault
Marketing and selling with fonts bold
But statuary warning printed in miniscule

O dear Government! Warning is not suffice
Close the injurious industry is the goodwill choice.
You earn revenue through so many taxes
Your coffers have no lexes
You posses the power to reign
Do not misuse it on the voters in bargain
Cancer does not discriminate
Do not think O Bureaucrats! That to you it hates.

Cancer spares no one these days
Mouth, Bones, Blood are not spared

Adopt healthy food habits
Early to rise Early to bed advise

War against Cancer needs all hands.
Join you me O my Friends!

Readers' Reviews on her blog

"Circumstances play prism to bring out friendship hues
Those who grew up together
They not necessarily are birds of the same feather
One may be energetic extrovert
Other may be totally opposite cool introvert
Their bond is like blending red with blue."
Ved Sachar: Keep Writing, a Very Apt Flair for writing. So beautifully expressed. Be Blessed

"Just last night
With God I indulged in an argument forthright
To pacify myself and to know
And asked these questions in a row
"O Almighty Thou art the creator of this planet
Tell me then the formulae used in making Indian Army combatant."
Ved Sachar:" Very Very beautifully articulated the Saintly, Selfless Life of a soldier. Kudos
Ved Sachar So well expressed the True feelings of Armed Forces. A real appreciation

Reema Malhotra Sachdeva

"JAI GURUJI AUNTY

I am in love with your magnetic aura. Your pious soul attracted my soul towards you. When I first saw your post on Guruji group I loved reading it. I think you are writing or have written some book. There is something in you which knocked my soul and pulled me towards it. There is a strong urge in me from within to speak to you. This kind of experience I never had. I m sure there is something behind it. Some driving force and I really don't know what is it... wish to hear you aunty. Do reciprocate. Please give me your no."

Printed in the United States
By Bookmasters